JACK RAU

DISCOVERING THE
LOST MAYA CITIES

Eight Major Sites Described,
with Drawings and a Map
by the Artist-Author-Printer

THE CLASSIC MAYA
CALENDAR YEAR
12.17.6.9.17 1 Caban 0 Pop

Coordinated with
Christian Civil 1960-61

THE PRE-COLUMBIAN PRESS

NEW YORK

DEDICATION
J. B. L., C. H. T.,
P. *and* E. B.

ABOUT THE MAYA CITIES

FOR 2,000 YEARS, in a geographical isolation unique in the history of man, the Maya people developed the most extraordinary civilization in the New World. When the Spanish conquerors arrived in Mexico and Central America, the former cities had been abandoned, and the inhabitants reduced to a semi-primitive rural life.

Why? Conjectures are that succesive jungle areas, burned down and planted in corn, were exhausted, causing further removal from population centers. Prolonged drought, pestilence, internal political stress have been considered.

Archeological research is still uncovering the records of an amazing people, who developed agriculture, an astronomical calendar, a mathematical system using the zero and numerical value by relative position, hieroglyphic writing, folded books, rubber, pottery and carving, an architecture of stone and stucco— all without a knowledge of the wheel or beasts of burden.

This little book describes those archeological sites most accessible today: Tikal by air from Guatemala City; Chichen Itza and Uxmal by car from Merida; Kabah by car from Uxmal, and into the jungle by jeep to Sayil and Labna. Palenque is reached by charter plane, or train from Campeche (which lies beyond Kabah). A charter plane from Guatemala City or Tegucigalpa takes you to Copan in Honduras.

On watercolor trips I have tried to record the wonder of the Cities of the Mayas. I submit this first book from my new Press, to bring samples of my hobbies: art, travel, printing.

ABOUT THE CALENDAR

THE MAYA SYSTEM of "writing" was mainly ideographic with symbols expressing ideas, but there may have also been phonetic glyphs—one of the few systems of writing in pre-Columbian culture. Many Maya hieroglyphic inscriptions and three famous existing manuscripts furnish background details.

With the Spanish conquest, educated Mayas were taught by Catholic missionaries, learning to write of pre-conquest matters with Spanish letters. The Bishop of Yucatan, Fray Diego de Landa, made a mid-sixteenth century account in his famous *Relacion de las cosas de Yucatan*, 1566. In this first-hand observation, we have a description of the calendar, with translations of Maya glyphs for days and months.

To us, the Maya calendar seems complicated in containing both a sacred and a civil year.

Twenty day-names were numbered from 1 to 13, again and again, until every number had been attached to every name, 13×20 or 260 days, a *tzolkin* or sacred year.

The *haab*, or civil year, contained 18 months of 20 days each, and a closing month of 5 days: 18×20 or 360 days plus 5 days or 365 days. The haab and tzolkin were meshed. By this system only once in 52 years (a calendar round) would any number-day month-name coincide.

We have started this Calendar at our Friday, April 15, 1960. Here begins the Classic Maya "long count" year or Initial Series position, the glyphs which are placed at the beginning of an inscription, notated 12.17.6.9.17 1 Caban 0 Pop, and read 12 Baktun, 17 Katun, 6 Tun, 9 Uinal, 17 Kin, 1 Caban 0 Pop.

The Maya year did not provide for leap days, hours, minutes, nor seconds as we do, so correlation after nearly 400 years is complicated.

All archeologists do not agree, but our starting point is based on scholastic evidence. *Kan* is included in the first day of Landa's year (it is eight days later below). And, perhaps even now in the Highlands, years begin with *Ik*, which is six days later in this version of the calendar.

Also see page 31.

CLASSIC MAYA YEAR
12.17.6.9.17 1 CABAN 0 POP BEGINS

POP

Jaguar

Maya months were named for the gods of nature. Some can be identified.

1	Caban	*POP*	*APRIL 1960* Friday	15
2	Eznab		Saturday	16
3	Cauac		Sunday	17
4	Ahua		Monday	18
5	Imix		Tuesday	19
6	Ik		Wednesday	20
7	Akbal		Thursday	21
8	Kan		Friday	22
9	Chicchan		Saturday	23
10	Cimi		Sunday	24
11	Manik		Monday	25
12	Lamat		Tuesday	26
13	Muluc		Wednesday	27
1	Oc		Thursday	28
2	Chuen		Friday	29
3	Eb		Saturday	30

Area of Map

8

UO
God of
Number 7

ZIP
Serpent
God

4	Ben		*MAY* Sunday	1
5	Ix		Monday	2
6	Men		Tuesday	3
7	Cib		Wednesday	4
8	Caban	*UO*	Thursday	5
9	Eznab		Friday	6
10	Cauac		Saturday	7
11	Ahua		Sunday	8
12	Imix		Monday	9
13	Ik		Tuesday	10
1	Akbal		Wednesday	11
2	Kan		Thursday	12
3	Chicchan		Friday	13
4	Cimi		Saturday	14
5	Manik		Sunday	15
6	Lamat		Monday	16
7	Muluc		Tuesday	17
8	Oc		Wednesday	18
9	Chuen		Thursday	16
10	Eb		Friday	20
11	Ben		Saturday	21
12	Ix		Sunday	22
13	Men		Monday	23
1	Cib		Tuesday	24
2	Caban	*ZIP*	Wednesday	25
3	Eznab		Thursday	26
4	Cauac		Friday	27
5	Ahua		Saturday	28
6	Imix		Sunday	29
7	Ik		Monday	30
8	Akbal		Tuesday	31

9

Temple of the Giant Jaguar, Group I.

TIKAL, the jungle-overgrown city in the rain-forest, Peten, Guatemala, is possibly oldest and most extensive, and certainly has the highest edifice (229 feet) of the vanished Mayas. Here are temple groups, ballcourts and plazas, linked by causeways. The great size of this Temple, with chamber and roof-comb above, indicates the importance of the city. Jungle growth has torn the stonework, rain has bleached the stucco. Near-by, the tomb of a high priest, who died about 400 A.D., was recently found by archeologists.

ZOTZ
Bat

9 Kan	*JUNE*	Wednesday	1
10 Chicchan		Thursday	2
11 Cimi		Friday	3
12 Manik		Saturday	4
13 Lamat		Sunday	5
1 Muluc		Monday	6
2 Oc		Tuesday	7
3 Chuen		Wednesday	8
4 Eb		Thursday	9
5 Ben		Friday	10
6 Ix		Saturday	11
7 Men		Sunday	12
8 Cib		Monday	13
9 Caban	*ZOTZ*	Tuesday	14
10 Eznab		Wednesday	15
11 Cauac		Thursday	16
12 Ahua		Friday	17
13 Imix		Saturday	18
1 Ik		Sunday	19
2 Akbal		Monday	20
3 Kan		Tuesday	21
4 Chicchan		Wednesday	22
5 Cimi		Thursday	23
6 Manik		Friday	24
7 Lamat		Saturday	25
8 Muluc		Sunday	26
9 Oc		Monday	27
10 Chuen		Tuesday	28
11 Eb		Wednesday	29
12 Ben		Thursday	30

 TZEC
God of the
day Caban

 XUL

13 Ix		*JULY* Friday 1
1 Men		Saturday 2
2 Cib		Sunday 3
3 Caban	*TZEC*	Monday 4
4 Eznab		Tuesday 5
5 Cauac		Wednesday 6
6 Ahua		Thursday 7
7 Imix		Friday 8
8 Ik		Saturday 9
9 Akbal		Sunday 10
10 Kan		Monday 11
11 Chicchan		Tuesday 12
12 Cimi		Wednesday 13
13 Manik		Thursday 14
1 Lamat		Friday 15

Pyramid 78, in a park-like setting, is fronted by a row of stelae, each with an altar.   TIKAL

2	Muluc		Saturday	16
3	Oc		Sunday	17
4	Chuen		Monday	18
5	Eb		Tuesday	19
6	Ben		Wednesday	20
7	Ix		Thursday	21
8	Men		Friday	22
9	Cib		Saturday	23
10	Caban	*XUL*	Sunday	24
11	Eznab		Monday	25
12	Cauac		Tuesday	26
13	Ahua		Wednesday	27
1	Imix		Thursday	28
2	Ik		Friday	29
3	Akbal		Saturday	30
4	Kan		Sunday	31

The Great Pyramid (Castillo)   CHICHEN ITZA

IN YUCATAN the topsoil is thin. There are no lakes or surface rivers but a network of underground waterways. Sisal is extensively planted for the making of cordage, but at the height of the Maya civilization corn and other crops were grown to feed a vast population.

We can comfortably visit the Classic Maya cities which once served as centers for temples, palaces, ballcourts and sacred structures ruled by the nobility and priesthood.

From Merida, a series of major Maya archeological areas can be reached: Chichen Itza to the east, Uxmal to the west, and nearby Kabah, and jungle-hidden Sayil and Labna.

CHICHEN ITZA is 90 miles from Merida. One passes through native towns, sisal plantations, and suddenly the massive *Castillo* is sighted. In nine terraces, plus a temple, it has a height of 90 feet. There are 91-step stairs on all four sides.

YAXKIN
Sun

5	Chicchan	*AUGUST*	Monday 1
6	Cimi		Tuesday 2
7	Manik		Wednesday 3
8	Lamat		Thursday 4
9	Muluc		Friday 5
10	Oc		Saturday 6
11	Chuen		Sunday 7
12	Eb		Monday 8
13	Ben		Tuesday 9
1	Ix		Wednesday 10
2	Men		Thursday 11
3	Cib		Friday 12
4	Caban	*YAXKIN*	Saturday 13
5	Eznab		Sunday 14
6	Cauac		Monday 15
7	Ahua		Tuesday 16
8	Imix		Wednesday 17
9	Ik		Thursday 18
10	Akbal		Friday 19
11	Kan		Saturday 20
12	Chicchan		Sunday 21
13	Cimi		Monday 22
1	Manik		Tuesday 23
2	Lamat		Wednesday 24
3	Muluc		Thursday 25
4	Oc		Friday 26
5	Chuen		Saturday 27
6	Eb		Sunday 28
7	Ben		Monday 29
8	Ix		Tuesday 30
9	Men		Wednesday 31

The Nunnery and Iglesita (*Little Church*) *reveal evidence of Maya glory*   CHICHEN ITZA

A calendar symbol can be deducted: 91 times 4 makes 364, plus a top step to the platform common to all stairways or 365.

From the platform a lavish architecture is to be seen in every view. At the right, the Temple of the Warriors, in pyramid form, is bordered by the Temple of a Thousand Columns. Ahead is the causeway leading to the Well of Sacrifice, a *cenote* exposed when a thin limestone surface caved in ages ago, and from which gold objects and artifacts were dredged. At the left are the ceremonial Ballcourt and the adjoining Temple of Tigers, with vestiges of a scenic mural.

Across the Merida Highway are other buildings: see the Observatory or *Caracol* (snail), so called because of a spiral staircase, and with a construction so devised that movements of the stars could be charted to fix the Calendar; and nearby is the Nunnery, so called because of the numerous small chambers in convents.

To the south is Old Chichen, with interesting ruins and a completely restored Temple.

MOL

 CHEN
Moon

10 Cib	*SEPTEMBER*	Thursday	1
11 Caban	*MOL*	Friday	2
12 Eznab		Saturday	3
13 Cauac		Sunday	4
1 Ahua		Monday	5
2 Imix		Tuesday	6
3 Ik		Wednesday	7
4 Akbal		Thursday	8
5 Kan		Friday	9
6 Chicchan		Saturday	10
7 Cimi		Sunday	11
8 Manik		Monday	12
9 Lamat		Tuesday	13
10 Muluc		Wednesday	14
11 Oc		Thursday	15
12 Chuen		Friday	16
13 Eb		Saturday	17
1 Ben		Sunday	18
2 Ix		Monday	19
3 Men		Tuesday	20
4 Cib		Wednesday	21
5 Caban	*CHEN*	Thursday	22
6 Eznab		Friday	23
7 Cauac		Saturday	24
8 Ahua		Sunday	25
9 Imix		Monday	26
10 Ik		Tuesday	27
11 Akbal		Wednesday	28
12 Kan		Thursday	29
13 Chicchan		Friday	30

House of the Governor   UXMAL

UXMAL, 50 miles west of Merida, is the first of a chain of cities 20 miles long, including Kabah, Sayil and Labna. It comes into view from the Puuc hills, one of the few breaks in the flatness of Yucatan. When seen close by, it seems small. But there is charm in this concentrated effect. Outstanding is the Pyramid of the Magician,

YAX
Venus

1 Cimi	*OCTOBER*	Saturday	1
2 Manik		Sunday	2
3 Lamat		Monday	3
4 Muluc		Tuesday	4
5 Oc		Wednesday	5
6 Chuen		Thursday	6
7 Eb		Friday	7
8 Ben		Saturday	8
9 Ix		Sunday	9
10 Men		Monday	10
11 Cib		Tuesday	11
12 Caban	*YAX*	Wednesday	12
13 Eznab		Thursday	13
1 Cauac		Friday	14
2 Ahua		Saturday	15
3 Imix		Sunday	16
4 Ik		Monday	17
5 Akbal		Tuesday	18
6 Kan		Wednesday	19
7 Chicchan		Thursday	20
8 Cimi		Friday	21
9 Manik		Saturday	22
10 Lamat		Sunday	23
11 Muluc		Monday	24
12 Oc		Tuesday	25
13 Chuen		Wednesday	26
1 Eb		Thursday	27
2 Ben		Friday	28
3 Ix		Saturday	29
4 Men		Sunday	30
5 Cib		Monday	31

Facade, Temple of Masks   KABAH

100 feet high, and steep. From the top one can look down into the Courtyard of the Nuns. To our left is the House of the Governor, 300 feet long. A sculptured frieze encircles the building; doorways break the front; the rear has niches of corbeled arches in which sloping walls converge until the space is spanned by a single slab.

KABAH, the fortress of Uxmal, for protection from the south, contains fine examples of Maya stone work: see the 150-foot long facade of the Temple of the Masks, covered with a repeated

ZAC
*God of the
Uinal or 20-
day period*

 CEH
New Fire

6 Caban	*ZAC*	*NOVEMBER*	Tuesday 1
7 Eznab			Wednesday 2
8 Cauac			Thursday 3
9 Ahua			Friday 4
10 Imix			Saturday 5
11 Ik			Sunday 6
12 Akbal			Monday 7
13 Kan			Tuesday 8
1 Chicchan			Wednesday 9
2 Cimi			Thursday 10
3 Manik			Friday 11
4 Lamat			Saturday 12
5 Muluc			Sunday 13
6 Oc			Monday 14
7 Chuen			Tuesday 15
8 Eb			Wednesday 16
9 Ben			Thursday 17
10 Ix			Friday 18
11 Men			Saturday 19
12 Cib			Sunday 20
13 Caban	*CEH*		Monday 21
1 Eznab			Tuesday 22
2 Cauac			Wednesday 23
3 Ahua			Thursday 24
4 Imix			Friday 25
5 Ik			Saturday 26
6 Akbal			Sunday 27
7 Kan			Monday 28
8 Chicchan			Tuesday 29
9 Cimi			Wednesday 30

Mask of Sun God, Palace   SAYIL

pattern of the open-mouth Rain God. On both
sides of the Highway are interesting buildings,
pyramids, and the remains of an arch. The stone
decoration, characteristic of the Puuc area, is in
contrast to the stucco of other Maya cities.

SAYIL is deep in the scrub jungle back of Kabah,
and the jeep trip is memorable. One leaves from
Uxmal early in the morning, and after a short
visit to Kabah, you enter the jungle road. The
way is not for the faint. Mid-morning, Sayil is
in view. Notable here are the dance platform, a
ballcourt, and a triple-terraced Palace, all richly
ornamented, and with indications of what was
once a grand staircase, leading from terrace to

MAC
A Young
God

 KANKIN

10 Manik	*DECEMBER*	Thursday 1
11 Lamat		Friday 2
12 Muluc		Saturday 3
13 Oc		Sunday 4
1 Chuen		Monday 5
2 Eb		Tuesday 6
3 Ben		Wednesday 7
4 Ix		Thursday 8
5 Men		Friday 9
6 Cib		Saturday 10
7 Caban	*MAC*	Sunday 11
8 Eznab		Monday 12
9 Cauac		Tuesday 13
10 Ahua		Wednesday 14
11 Imix		Thursday 15
12 Ik		Friday 16
13 Akbal		Saturday 17
1 Kan		Sunday 18
2 Chicchan		Monday 19
3 Cimi		Tuesday 20
4 Manik		Wednesday 21
5 Lamat		Thursday 22
6 Muluc		Friday 23
7 Oc		Saturday 24
8 Chuen		Sunday 25
9 Eb		Monday 26
10 Ben		Tuesday 27
11 Ix		Wednesday 28
12 Men		Thursday 29
13 Cib		Friday 30
1 Caban	*KANKIN*	Saturday 31

23

The unique Arch LABNA

terrace. Sayil flourished during the classic period, but ceased civic activities and the erection
of elaborate buildings, and about 894 A.D. was
finally abandoned.

LABNA is finally reached. The area is park-like,
and restoration can be observed in progress. As
a ceremonial city, Labna was contemporaneous
with Kabah and Sayil, and the ninth century
marks its height of occupancy and influence.
There is a spreading Great Palace, with many
rooms. A sculpture depicts a human head as
emerging from the jaws of a conventionalized
serpent. Most notable is an arched Gateway, as
restored. Rich in geometric pattern, there are
miniatures of the typical thatch-roofed Maya
houses worked into the facade.

MUAN
A young god

2 Eznab	*JANUARY, 1961*	Sunday 1
3 Cauac		Monday 2
4 Ahua		Tuesday 3
5 Imix		Wednesday 4
6 Ik		Thursday 5
7 Akbal		Friday 6
8 Kan		·Saturday 7
9 Chicchan		Sunday 8
10 Cimi		Monday 9
11 Manik		Tuesday 10
12 Lamat		Wednesday 11
13 Muluc		Thursday 12
1 Oc		Friday 13
2 Chuen		Saturday 14
3 Eb		Sunday 15
4 Ben		Monday 16
5 Ix		Tuesday 17
6 Men		Wednesday 18
7 Cib		Thursday 19
8 Caban	*MUAN*	Friday 20
9 Eznab		Saturday 21
10 Cauac		Sunday 22
11 Ahua		Monday 23
12 Imix		Tuesday 24
13 Ik		Wednesday 25
1 Akbal		Thursday 26
2 Kan		Friday 27
3 Chicchan		Saturday 28
4 Cimi		Sunday 29
5 Manik		Monday 30
6 Lamat		Tuesday 31

Temple of the Inscriptions

PALENQUE, serene and spacious, on a terrace backed by towering mountains, was one of the last of the Maya cities. Stucco workmanship is here to be seen at its height of perfection.

There are many pyramid-temples in the area, and the roof combs are unique.

The Palace, with many rooms, galleries and cellars, has a curious three-story tower. Opposite rises the Temple of Inscriptions, wherein a long hieroglyphic carving was discovered. But most notable is the crypt. It was deduced that holes in a floor slab were catches, and when the slab was lifted a rubble-filled stairway was discovered. When cleared, down the steep steps, a vault was found at ground level. The walls were decorated, and the sarcophagus of a noble was found under a magnificently carved monolith.

PAX

7	Muluc	*FEBRUARY*	Wednesday 1
8	Oc		Thursday 2
9	Chuen		Friday 3
10	Eb		Saturday 4
11	Ben		Sunday 5
12	Ix		Monday 6
13	Men		Tuesday 7
1	Cib		Wednesday 8
2	Caban	*PAX*	Thursday 9
3	Eznab		Friday 10
4	Cauac		Saturday 11
5	Ahua		Sunday 12
6	Imix		Monday 13
7	Ik		Tuesday 14
8	Akbal		Wednesday 15
9	Kan		Thursday 16
10	Chicchan		Friday 17
11	Cimi		Saturday 18
12	Manik		Sunday 19
13	Lamat		Monday 20
1	Muluc		Tuesday 21
2	Oc		Wednesday 22
3	Chuen		Thursday 23
4	Eb		Friday 24
5	Ben		Saturday 25
6	Ix		Sunday 26
7	Men		Monday 27
8	Cib		Tuesday 28

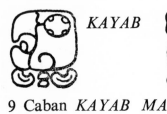 *KAYAB*   *CUMHU*

9 Caban *KAYAB*	*MARCH*	Wednesday 1
10 Eznab		Thursday 2
11 Cauac		Friday 3
12 Ahua		Saturday 4
13 Imix		Sunday 5
1 Ik		Monday 6
2 Akbal		Tuesday 7
3 Kan		Wednesday 8
4 Chicchan		Thursday 9
5 Cimi		Friday 10
6 Manik		Saturday 11
7 Lamat		Sunday 12
8 Muluc		Monday 13
9 Oc		Tuesday 14
10 Chuen		Wednesday 15

28

The Palace and its unique tower, as viewed from the Temple of Inscriptions.   PALENQUE

11	Eb		Thursday 16
12	Ben		Friday 17
13	Ix		Saturday 18
1	Men		Sunday 19
2	Cib		Monday 20
3	Caban	*CUMHU*	Tuesday 21
4	Eznab		Wednesday 22
5	Cauac		Thursday 23
6	Ahua		Friday 24
7	Imix		Saturday 25
8	Ik		Sunday 26
9	Akbal		Monday 27
10	Kan		Tuesday 28
11	Chicchan		Wednesday 29
12	Cimi		Thursday 30
13	Manik		Friday 31

The Hieroglyph Stairway   COPAN

COPAN, near the Honduras-Guatemala border, is a greenish stone city of pyramids and terraces, plazas and courts, temples and altars, all shaded by giant ceiba trees. It was one of the first great Maya centers of learning, and, geographically, the south-east rampart of the civilization.

There are sculptured monuments of human figures, with dedication-date glyphs ranging 460 to 800 A.D. One temple was dedicated 756, on the discovery by the astronomer-priests of the time intervals between eclipses.

A river has eroded the Acropolis, to leave a cross-section of earlier floor levels in view. An earthquake telescoped the sculptured steps of the Stairway, which has been restored. But the original sequence of the hieroglyphics has been lost forever.

UAYEB
North Star

1 Lamat	*APRIL*	Saturday	1
2 Muluc		Sunday	2
3 Oc		Monday	3
4 Chuen		Tuesday	4
5 Eb		Wednesday	5
6 Ben		Thursday	6
7 Ix		Friday	7
8 Men		Saturday	8
9 Cib		Sunday	9
10 Caban	*UAYEB*	Monday	10
11 Eznab	*The Five*	Tuesday	11
12 Cauac	*Days*	Wednesday	12
13 Ahua	*of*	Thursday	13
1 Imix	*Misfortune*	Friday	14

MORE ABOUT THE CALENDAR

THE DAYS of Misfortune, the five added days of *Uayeb*, brought the civil year, 18 months of 20 days each, more nearly in line with the solar calendar. These days were considered unlucky, continence was observed,all work was avoided.

But the Maya knew that their 365-day year lacked a quarter day of a true solar year. Without a leap year, they corrected the accumulated error every 20 years when erecting a stelae.

The Maya calendar concept, known used as early as 618 B.C., must surely be man's earliest piece of systematic science.

This is the first book published by
The Pre-Columbian Press.

The hand-set type is
Monotype Times Roman.
The paper is Curtis Colophon Text.
The hand press is a Columbian No. 2.
Binding by Practical Bookbinding Co., Inc.

Limited edition, 500 copies.